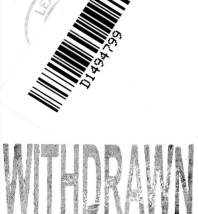

This book is dedicated
to
Kevin Jacobsen (1933 - 2005)

Jacobsen was a visionary and a man of many talents. He was an fisherman, filmmaker, and an experienced Living Food chef.

Jacobsen in Copenhagen, he came to Ireland in his early twenties, by the portrait of Ireland in the film 'The Quiet Man'.

ed about Inishere from a fellow Dane living in Dublin and made the his picturesque island.

simply with the islanders, supporting himself through catching and eels. While there, he became intrigued with Catholicism and made the decision to become a Catholic. He took the name 'Kevin', after the local saint.

After some time, he founded the Catholic Community 'the Servants of Love'*.

As a result of personal illness in later years, Kevin became interested in healthy eating. Creating healthy food turned out to be a passion in Kevin's life. He travelled to restaurants in America to learn and experience the art of making raw food taste delicious. As a result, when he returned, he invented machinery to produce the food. His dream was to open a Living Food (Raw) cafe, a task which he was in the process of doing when he died.

The cafe is now open and is called the 'Healthy Habits Cafe'.

This book contains many of his recipes.

* www.theservantsoflove.com

1

S.O.L. Productions Ltd.,
Quarantine Hill,
Wicklow Town,
Ireland
Tel: +353 (0)404 68645
Fax: +353 (0)404 67153
www.healthyhabs.com

Photographs © Paul Diamond
unless otherwise stated

Cover, Art and Design: Veronica O'Reilly
Edited by Gabrielle Kirby

First published hardback © 2009 S.O.L. Productions Ltd.
Published by S.O.L. Productions Ltd.
© 2012 S.O.L. Productions Ltd.

Measurements
In this book, quantities are given in metric and imperial measures.
Metric measures have been rounded off to nearest workable figures.

Example: 1 ounce, or 28 g, works at 25 g
             1 pint, or 567 ml, works at 600 ml

My 'Spoon' Measurements

1 teaspoon   =   5 ml
1 dessertspoon =   10 ml
1 tablespoon   =   17.7 ml

In this book, 1 cup = 100g (same as USA)

(For reference... USA tablespoon = 14.2 ml   Australian tablespoon = 20 ml)

Veronica O'Reilly asserts the moral right to be identified
as the author of this work.
ISBN 978-1-90171-224-7

Acknowledgements

This book is a combined effort of the Servants of Love Community and friends.

It has been inspired by Kevin Jacobsen. His passion for making healthy food taste delicious led him to experiment until he discovered the 'right' taste. The food had to have texture, taste and great presentation.

Kevin and I travelled to Los Angeles, San Francisco, Las Vegas and New York to get some experience of Living Food preparation and to develop our palate.

I wish to thank all the great chefs who helped us - Ito from Au Lac Restaurant, Ursula from Good Mood Cafe, Juliano, Eddie and Lily from Raw Soul, Chad Sarno and many more.

A big 'thank you' also to Deirdre McCafferty who agreed to write the introduction in the middle of her busy life, Bernadette Bohan for a laugh and encouragement, Yvonne Gorman for listening, Clare Hickey for reading the recipes, Mary Lou Byrne for sharing her chef's experience with me, and Máirín O'Donovan Thermes. Thanks also to all the students and customers for their support.

A special thanks to my community - Gabrielle Kirby, a great editor, Paul Diamond for his beautiful photography and Seamus, Bernard, Vera, Maura and Michaela for their support, interest and love.

A final thanks to my family - Bill, Terry and their families for their continued belief in me and to my brother Johnny who passed away before this book was completed.

Veronica O'Reilly

Introduction

By Deirdre McCafferty
proprietor of Cornucopia Vegetarian Restaurant
and member of Alive – the Irish Living Food Association.

It is a great honour to have been asked by Veronica O'Reilly to write the introduction to her recipe book of living foods "Raw In A Cold Climate". Veronica is a very talented chef and she has that very special gift of creating exceptionally tasty food, that certain "Je ne sais quoi?" that makes her dishes "sing". It is wonderful to eat healthy food, but it is even more glorious if that food is also very delicious and beautifully presented. Offered within the following pages are 75 living food/raw recipes for soups, salads, main courses, sauces, and desserts. Enjoy!

A dedication and a journey

At the request of Veronica this book is dedicated to visionary, Catholic monk and founder of the community 'Servants Of Love', Kevin Jacobson (1933 to 2005). I first met Kevin in Wicklow Town in 2002 when he told me of his passion for living food, i.e. vegan, uncooked food that is both life-enhancing and healing. He also told me about his ambition to set up an organisation and indeed a restaurant where living foods could be both taught and experienced. Kevin was not a man to "let moss grow under his feet" and, though in his mid 70's, in January 2004 he set off to the United States "to learn information from other tribes and to bring it back to our tribe". Veronica, also of the same community, accompanied him, and armed with a small budget they went on an adventure and a journey throughout the United States from New York to San Francisco. They volunteered their catering services, learning from and working with talented chefs in living foods restaurants - Raw Soul in New York, Juliano's in Los Angeles, and Ito of Au Lac. They came home with tales of adventure and (most importantly) recipes, information and inspiration, and set to fine-tuning and adapting these recipes to the Irish climate and palate. This recipe book "Raw In A Cold Climate" is the brainchild born out of that inspirational journey.

Alive

Alive – the Irish Living Foods Association was founded in 2003. Once again, Kevin Jacobsen was the main impetus behind its creation. Alive is an organisation that provides information and guidance for anyone seeking to improve their health and lifestyle. For the past five years we have had a monthly talk and "party" followed by a living foods dinner. This has been a source of fun, information, inspiration and delicious food for all attending. Information on upcoming talks, on recipes, juicers, sprouting, wheatgrass, etc. is available on our web-site www.irishlivingfoods.com.

Living foods

What are Living foods? These are vegetarian plant-based dishes where the freshest of ingredients are presented and prepared in a manner that preserves the naturally occurring enzymes and vitamins vital for digestion. Enzymes and vitamins are damaged when food reaches temperatures of over 43°C. Raw and Living foods are also always vegetarian and vegan/plant based. They exact very little strain on the body when it comes to digestion and encourage the body towards a more alkaline and less acidic state. More and more studies show that the human body heals well when being nourished by this type of food. Immunity is boosted and energy and feelings of well-being are enhanced.

How to prepare food that is tasty was the task which Kevin and Veronica set themselves. They were determined that when changing recipes from cooked ones to raw ones or when creating new raw recipes that there be no compromise in taste, texture and presentation.

Healthy Habits Restaurant

Kevin and Veronica put their whole hearts into creating the most tasty and delicious recipes without compromising the health and vitality of the dishes. They succeeded and we, their friends, benefited greatly. All of these dishes, as well as many other recipes that have been created and collected by Veronica herself, are now available in the restaurant "Healthy Habits" which opened its doors in June 2007 in Wicklow Town, and has been delighting visitors far and wide with its tasty dishes.

Raw In A Cold Climate

Despite the untimely loss of Kevin Jacobsen in 2005, Veronica continued in her ambition to write this excellent recipe book, which I know Kevin would be most proud of. As already stated, Veronica is especially talented in the creation of mouth-watering living food recipes. Her soups, salads, main courses, desserts, sauces and pâtés are truly delicious to the taste buds and enlivening to the health of the body and the mind. She has an expertise with dehydrator, blender, knife, juicer, sprouter, mandolin and, of course, with the fruit, vegetables, beans, seeds, nuts, grains, herbs, oils and natural sweeteners which are the raw materials of her culinary works of art.

We hope you, the reader, will incorporate many of these recipes into your daily fare and that new energy will enhance your life. I know Kevin would be very happy with the creation of this book and with its 75 different Living Food recipes.

"A healthy Immune System protects you from much suffering, worry and expense. The danger is that we take it for granted because, when it's working well, we don't notice it." *Kevin Jacobsen*

Author's Note

I have been the cook in our community, the Servants of Love*, for over twenty years. During that time, I cooked mainly traditional food - meat and two vegetables. At one stage we lived in Roundstone, where we had our own cows which we hand-milked. I made butter and Ymer - a Danish milk-based dish not unlike yogurt - and also Ice Cream.

We were developing our automatic Long Line Fishing System at the time so I had a lot of fish coming in as well.

I collected seaweed (Dulse) from the shoreline around our 30 acres of land and used it to make Colcannon. Our founder, Kevin, became ill with angina and his diet had to change. So did ours.

As the years passed, and we moved to Wicklow, our outlook on food changed. Food could be helpful in maintaining good quality health. Through a lot of research we became more aware of the importance of diet. We then discovered, through a friend, Raw Food. Kevin became immediately interested and began growing wheatgrass, sprouting seeds and preparing raw dishes.

My first grasp of Raw Food Preparation came when I attended Chad Sarno's course in London. I learned how tasty the dishes could be and how easy they were to prepare. Thus began a new adventure for Kevin and I as we prepared our dishes.

Love is the most important ingredient in preparing food. Love everything you touch, make or create. Putting love into everything is the secret behind a great dish.

The recipes in this book are the result of our quest for the perfect bite. All ingredients can be sourced in Ireland and the recipes are in metric and imperial.

Always have the plates and bowls warm. This gives that comfort feeling which we need in a cold climate. Warm soups are a must. Entrées may be placed in the dehydrator** for 30 minutes to 'warm up'. Presentation is important, but taste is of paramount importance. Work on taste and presentation. Food is one of the most delicate areas of personal choice.

Have fun and experiment, experiment and experiment!

Veronica

Table of Contents

Launch of Healthy Habits Cafe 17th June 2007

Johnny O'Reilly & Seamus Byrne

Vera Walsh, Larry & Doris Keegan, Margaret Doyle

Joshua Kelly

Gabrielle Kirby and Deirdre McCafferty

Johnny, Chiara and Karen

Melon is a delicious, cooling and refreshing start to any meal. It's one of my favourites. Enjoy.

MINTY MELON

½ watermelon
½ galia melon
½ honeydew
mint

Remove the seeds from the melons.
Remove rind.
Dice into bite size pieces and put into a bowl.
Chop mint finely and add to the melons.
Stir and allow to stand for at least 30 minutes.
Refrigerate and serve chilled.

Serves 4 - 6

Preparation time: 15 minutes

I like serving flax crackers with soup. They're very versatile. Make enough for a few weeks. Store in airtight containers.

FLAX CRACKERS

300 g / 12 oz flax seeds
3 medium red onions
3 medium tomatoes
2 teaspoons dried basil
sea salt to taste

Barely cover flax seeds with water. Leave overnight.
Next day, stir and add more water if mixture is dry. Leave aside, stirring occasionally. Third day, chop onions and tomatoes finely, add to flax mixture. Mix well and add seasonings.
Place mixture on a teflex* sheet or a non-stick drying sheet.
Cover loosely with parchment or a large freezer bag to prevent mixture sticking to rolling pin.
Roll to size of dehydrator** sheet (3 mm thickness).
Remove the parchment/freezer bag. Trim edges and, using a knife, score the mixture to mark out 12 square crackers.
Place on dehydrator** shelf (or shelves) and dehydrate for 12 hours at 42°c/115°f when it should be ready to turn over and remove the teflex* sheet.
Continue to dehydrate for 4 more hours.
Break apart when thoroughly dry. Store in an airtight container.

HERB CRACKERS

200 g / 8 oz flax seeds
2½ red onions
1 medium red pepper
1 medium yellow pepper
2 dessertspoons dried basil
2 teaspoons dried oregano
sea salt to taste

Follow the method for Flax Crackers.   *Preparation time: 1 hour.*

* page 120, ** page 120

Avocado adds a little extra something to a meal.
A dip like this can make a snack into a very easy lunch!

AVOCADO DIP

1 avocado
1 clove garlic
1 dessertspoon Bragg Aminos*, seasoning or tamari**
1 teaspoon lemon juice

Peel avocado and mix with the seasoning.

Serve with crudités*** or on flax crackers.
Use same day.

Preparation time: 5 minutes.

'CHEESE' SPREAD

200 g / 8 oz pine nuts (soaked 3 hours approx. and drained)
50 g / 2 oz sundried tomatoes soaked for 2 hours
½ red and ½ yellow pepper
1 dessertspoon lemon juice
1 clove garlic minced

Blend all ingredients.
Serve on crackers.

Preparation time:
15 minutes.

* page 124, ** page 127, *** page 125

These 'crisps' are a great treat when watching TV.

'CRISPS`

1 parsnip
1 yam
1 carrot
1 beetroot
A little lemon juice

Spice Mix
salt to taste
1 dessertspoon onion powder
½ teaspoon cayenne pepper.

Make spice mix, add lemon juice and leave aside.
Prepare vegetables.
Peel vegetables with a wide peeler into crisp-like pieces.
Massage spice mix into vegetables.
Put onto the teflex* sheet and dehydrate for 8 hours or until crisp.
Half-way through, flip over.
Serve right away or keep in an airtight container.

Preparation time: 25 minutes.

* page 120

Sunflower Paté was one of Kevin's first recipes. This one is a great everyday spread. Sun Corn Paté is a lovely treat.

SUNFLOWER PATÉ

Soak 100 g / 4 oz sunflower seeds for 2 hours.
Drain and discard water.

Blend in a blender with a little water. Place in a muslin bag.
Allow to drain for a few hours.
When firm to the touch, place mixture in a bowl or blender and add...

1 dessertspoon olive oil
½ dessertspoon Bragg Aminos*/tamari**
¼ teaspoon mild chilli powder
dash cayenne pepper
1 teaspoon lemon juice
salt to taste

Blend and serve as a dip or paste.
Best kept in fridge and used within three days.

Preparation time: 15 minutes (after sunflower paste has drained).

SUN CORN PATÉ

100 g / 4 oz sunflower seeds soaked for 2 hours and drained
200 g / 8 oz frozen or fresh corn
zest of ½ lemon
2 dessertspoons onion powder (or a little chopped onion)
1 teaspoon dried dill and sea salt to taste

In a food processor,
using the 'S' blade,
process all ingredients
together.
Adjust seasonings.
Serve on crackers.
Use within 2 days.

appetizers

Preparation time: 15 minutes.

* page 124, ** page 127

These lovely crispbreads are welcome with soup or paté.
I like using them as a base for burgers.

SUNFLOWER FLAX CRISPBREAD

400 g / 1 lb sunflower seeds
100 g / 4 oz flax seeds
2 dessertspoon flaxmeal*
salt to taste

Barely cover flax seeds with water.
Leave overnight.
Soak the sunflower seeds for 2 hours.
In a food processor, using a 'S' blade, process the flax seeds and sunflower seeds.
Add the flaxmeal* and salt.
Place mixture on a teflex** sheet or a non-stick drying sheet.
Cover loosely with parchment or a large freezer bag to prevent mixture sticking to rolling pin.
Roll to size of dehydrator*** sheet (3 mm thickness).
Remove the parchment/freezer bag.
Trim edges and, using a knife, score the mixture to mark out 12 square crackers.
Place on dehydrator*** shelf (or shelves) and dehydrate for 12 hours at 42°c/115°f when it should be ready to turn over and remove the teflex** sheet.
Continue to dehydrate for 4 more hours.
Break apart when thoroughly dry. Store in an airtight container.

Note: If you would like sweet crispbread, simply add 2 or 3 dessertspoons of agave**** syrup.

If you would like a thicker crispbread, roll them to your desired thickness and score. Dehydrate until thoroughly dry.

Preparation time: 1 hour.

appetizers

When Kevin and I were in Las Vegas, we visited 'Go Raw' in Smith's Shopping Center and, through them, we learned how to make wraps pliable. As soon as we camehome, Kevin experimented until he came up with this recipe.

KEVIN'S WRAPS

2 kg / 4½ lb carrots
1 kg / 2¼ lb apples
500 g / 13 oz golden flax seeds

Wash and peel vegetables and cut into small pieces.
Using the grater in a food processor, grate the carrots and apples and leave aside.
Next, process the mixture in the food processor using the 'S' blade.
Grind flax seeds and add to mixture.
Mix well to form a dough.
Place mixture on a teflex* sheet or a non-stick drying sheet the size of a dehydrator** shelf.
Cover loosely with parchment or a large freezer bag to prevent mixture sticking to rolling pin.
Roll to size of dehydrator** sheet (3 mm thickness).
Remove the parchment/freezer bag. Trim edges.
Place on dehydrator** shelves.
Dehydrate for 12 hours at 42°c/115°f.
Check if thoroughly dry. Score into 4 pieces and store in fridge.
(This recipe is for a 9 tray Excalabur Dehydrator.)
May substitute courgettes for apples.

appetizers

Preparation time:
90 minutes.

appetizers

These crunchies are lovely to snack on at any time.
I sometimes make a cereal out of them and add
sesame or almond milk. A very tasty breakfast!

BUCK CRUNCHIES

200 g / 8 oz buckwheat*
2 dessertspoons agave** syrup
1 dessertspoon cinnamon

Soak the buckwheat for fifteen minutes.
Drain, rinsing well.
In food processor, using the 'S' blade, combine the buckwheat*,
agave** and cinnamon.
Pulse a few times, making sure it remains crunchy.
Spread evenly on a teflex*** sheet.
Dehydrate 12 hours at 42°c/115°f.
Turn and continue dehydrating until crunchy.
Store in an airtight container. Use as a snack or cereal.

Preparation time: 15 minutes.

Variations
For a sweet, vanilla taste, add more agave** and ½ teaspoon
vanilla essence.
Experiment. This is a fun dish.

* page 124, ** page 124, *** page 120

These nuts are lovely to take with you when travelling.

SAVOURY NUTS

400 g / 16 oz almonds soaked overnight
2 dessertspoons olive oil
1 dessertspoon tamari* (optional)
½ teaspoon mild chilli powder
¼ teaspoon cumin

Drain the nuts and pat dry.
Make a mix of the spices, oil and tamari*.
Put the nuts into the mix and leave for about 1 hour.
Spread evenly on a teflex** sheet.
Dehydrate 12 hours at 42°c/115°f.
Turn and continue dehydrating until crunchy.
Store in an airtight container. Use as a snack.

Preparation time: 15 minutes.

Experiment with different types of nuts or seeds and seasonings.

This soup is what I would call a traditional country soup. Lovely on a cold, wet, windy day.

HEARTY LENTIL SOUP (Serves 4 - 6)

200 g / 8 oz sprouted lentils (soak overnight, drain, rinse morning and evening for 1 - 2 days).
Store in fridge.

1 medium onion chopped finely
2 sticks celery chopped finely
2 medium carrots diced
5 medium tomatoes chopped finely.

Fill a saucepan with 1½ litres of warm filtered water.
Place all the vegetables (not the lentils) in it and bring to a temperature of 42°c/115°f, stirring occasionally.

Stock
2 dessertspoons tamari*
2 dessertspoons olive oil
1 teaspoon sea salt or to taste
1 dessertspoon mixed herbs
1 teaspoon cumin
3 cloves garlic minced
300 ml / ½ pint filtered water
Blend all stock ingredients together and add to the vegetables, stirring occasionally while keeping the temperature at 42°c/115°f.
When vegetables are softened (about 1 hour) add the lentils.
Serve and enjoy. Suitable for freezing.

Preparation time: 25 minutes.

Sprouting Jars

soups

This is a great winter soup. Very welcoming on a cold day.

BROCCOLI & CASHEW/ALMOND SOUP   (Serves 4)

1 head of broccoli
100 g / 4 oz cashew (or almond) nuts soaked overnight
2 teaspoons lemon juice
sea salt to taste
¼ teaspoon cayenne pepper
750 ml / 1¼ pints filtered water
3 dessertspoons white miso* (shiro)
2 dessertspoons tamari**
3 dessertspoons onion powder (or a little
   chopped onion)

Marinade for Broccoli Florets
1 teaspoon lemon juice
2 dessertspoons olive oil
pinch of sea salt.

Wash broccoli and trim off outer tough skin of stem.
Part of the stem can be used for the stock.
Break the florets into small pieces and place in a bowl.
Pour marinade over the pieces and massage gently.
Leave aside.

To make stock, blend nuts, some of the filtered water and
rest of the ingredients in a blender until smooth.
Pause now and again to allow the machine to rest.
Add the remaining filtered water and blend.
Adjust seasonings to taste.
Pour into a saucepan and heat slowly, stirring occasionally.
Add the broccoli florets.
Heat to a temperature of 42°c/115°f.

Serve in warm bowls. Suitable for freezing.

Preparation time: 25 minutes.

* page 126, ** page 127

soups

I invented this soup because I was late preparing lunch for the community one day and the weather was cold.
It literally takes only 5 minutes.
Very handy if you are coming home from work and want something straight away.

ASIAN SEA SOUP   (1 person)

2 dessertspoons dulse* flakes
¼ diced red pepper
¼ diced yellow pepper
2 dessertspoons grated creamed coconut
¼ diced avocado
fresh basil

In a bowl place dulse*, coconut, peppers and avocado.
Leave aside.

Stock
150 ml / ¼ pint warm filtered water (hand hot)
2 teaspoons cold pressed sesame oil
1 dessertspoon tamari**
sea salt to taste

Blend and pour into the bowl.
Garnish with basil and serve immediately.

Preparation time: 5 minutes.

* page 125, ** page 127

soups

This soup is very warming and a great favourite with the community.

WARM CARROT SOUP   (Serves 4)

300 ml / ½ pint carrot juice
150 ml / ¼ pint coconut milk*
150 ml / ¼ pint filtered water
100 g / 4 oz cashew nuts soaked overnight
1 dessertspoon onion powder (or a little chopped onion)
1 teaspoon cumin
¾ teaspoon salt (optional)
¼ teaspoon cayenne pepper
½ teaspoon curry
1 teaspoon lime juice
1 dessertspoon tamari**
1 bunch fresh coriander

Blend the cashew nuts with some of the carrot juice until smooth.
Pause now and again to allow the machine to rest.
Add rest of juice, coconut milk, water and all the other ingredients.
Blend.
Pour into a saucepan and heat slowly, stirring occasionally.
Heat to a temperature of 42°c/115°f.
Serve in warm bowls. Use same day.

Note: May substitute 1 avocado for nuts.

Preparation time: 35 minutes.

This exotic soup brings all the flavours of the east together for you to enjoy.

THAI COCONUT SOUP (Serves 4)

50 g / 2 oz broccoli florets
25 g / 1 oz sliced mushrooms (optional)
100 g / 4 oz diced carrot
1 scallion chopped
1 bunch of coriander

Stock
450 ml / ¾ pint coconut milk*
1 dessertspoon lime juice
1 clove garlic minced
1 dessertspoon diced ginger
½ red chilli pepper seeded and diced
3 dessertspoons tamari**
3 teaspoons lemon grass finely chopped
50 g / 2 oz cashew nuts soaked overnight (optional)

Make the stock using a blender and pour into a saucepan.
Heat slowly and add vegetables. Check for taste and add
salt and water if needed.
Heat to a temperature of 42°c/115°f, stirring occasionally.
Serve in warm bowls.

Keeps for 2 days in fridge.

Preparation time: 35 minutes.

* page 102, ** page 127

soups

soups

I love mushrooms. It took me a long time to invent this raw mushroom soup. It's yummy.

MUSHROOM SOUP

100 g / 4 oz mushrooms
Juice of 6 celery sticks
75 g / 3 oz cashew nuts soaked for 6 - 8 hours or overnight
1 dessertspoon onion powder (or add a little chopped onion)
½ teaspoon sea salt or to taste
2 dessertspoons white miso* (shiro)
½ teaspoon tamari**
450 ml / ¾ pint filtered water
parsley

Drain cashew nuts and discard water.
Clean mushrooms with a damp cloth and slice.
Leave aside.
Pour the celery juice into a blender and add the cashew nuts, onion powder, salt, miso* and tamari**.
Add some of the filtered water and blend.
Pour into a saucepan. Add remaining filtered water and mushrooms.
Heat to a temperature of 42°c/115°f stirring occasionally.
Serve in warm bowls and sprinkle with fresh parsley.

Tip
For a thicker soup, blend the mushrooms.

Preparation time: 25 minutes.

* page 126, ** page 127

This salad is delicious in autumn, just before winter creeps in.

BROCCOLI & TOMATO SALAD

1 head of broccoli
3 medium tomatoes
fresh basil

Dressing
2 dessertspoons avocado oil (or olive oil)
1 dessertspoon onion powder
¼ teaspoon salt or to taste
1 teaspoon lemon juice.

Wash the vegetables.
Break the broccoli into bite-size pieces.
Dice the tomatoes and add to the broccoli.
Mix the ingredients for the dressing together.
Pour the dressing over the vegetables and massage
gently for about 10 minutes.
Serve.

Preparation time: 25 minutes.

Renee Sheane
Photograph by Genna Patterson B.A.

This is a salad with a difference. It's ideal in winter, as a lot of heat is brought to it by the chilli. It looks amazing.

LEMON CHILLI SLAW

100 g / 4 oz savoy cabbage shredded
50 g / 2 oz mange tout
1 stalk celery
1 red apple
1 scallion diced

Dressing
1 teaspoon agave* syrup or honey
3 dessertspoons olive oil
½ dessertspoon lemon juice
½ long red chilli pepper deseeded and diced

Cut the mange tout, celery and apple into julienne** strips and mix together in a bowl.
Blend the ingredients for the dressing in a blender and pour over vegetables.

Allow to marinate for at least 30 minutes before serving. Enjoy.

Preparation time: 20 minutes.

salads

salads

These sweet salads can be eaten every day.
They are ideal for children.

BEETROOT SALAD

200 g / 8 oz beetroot
1 medium apple
juice of ¼ lemon

Peel beetroot and apples.
Grate finely in a food processor or by hand.
Mix well and add lemon juice. Serve.

Tip
Add a little honey or agave* syrup for a sweeter flavour.

Preparation time: 20 minutes.

CARROT SALAD

200 g / 8 oz carrot
savoury seeds (soaked and dehydrated)

Peel carrots.
Grate them coarsely in a food processor or by hand.
Add seeds.
Mix well with french dressing**.
Serve.

Preparation time: 20 minutes.

* page 124, ** page 58

salads

This salad can be made all year round.
It's bright, cheery and delicious.

CAULIFLOWER SALAD   (Serves 2 - 4)

½ head cauliflower
½ red pepper
½ yellow pepper
3 medium tomatoes
chopped parsley

Marinade
2 dessertspoons filtered water
2 dessertspoons organic apple cider vinegar* or
lemon juice
2 dessertspoons organic agave** syrup or honey

Wash and cut the cauliflower into bite-size pieces.
Dice the peppers.
Slice the tomatoes thinly.
Place all the ingredients in a bowl.

Mix all the ingredients for the marinade together.
Pour marinade over the vegetables.
Allow to marinate for 30 minutes.

Serve sprinkled with chopped parsley.

Preparation time: 20 minutes.

I like this salad in winter, when it is difficult to face a salad. It's a substantial salad when the cold sets in and you need that extra kick.

FUSION MEDLEY SALAD

3 medium carrots, washed, peeled and cut into julienne*
strips
1 fennel bulb** cut into julienne* strips
1 head broccoli washed and broken into florets
a little red cabbage, shredded
1 red onion cut into thin rings
small bunch of fresh parsley chopped finely
2 medium red apples cut into julienne* strips (optional)

Marinade
4 dessertspoons olive oil
2 dessertspoons lemon juice
½ teaspoon grated fresh ginger
1 clove garlic minced

Blend all the ingredients for the marinade together and
allow to marinate for an hour.
Prepare the vegetables.
Pour marinade over the vegetables.
Allow to sit for at least 30 minutes before serving.

Serves 4

Preparation time: 20 minutes.

salads

* page 126, ** page 125

salads   salads   salads

The Green Simplicity Salad can be made with any green lettuce. It will compliment any dish. I often eat the Spinach Salad on its own, it's so tasty!

GREEN SIMPLICITY SALAD

butterhead lettuce
cos and green oakleaf lettuce
parsley, mint or any herb

Wash and dry lettuces.
Break into bite-size pieces into a bowl.
Chop herbs and add to bowl.
Drizzle french dressing* or your favourite dressing over the salad and serve.

Preparation time: 10 minutes.

SPINACH SALAD

125 g / 5 oz baby spinach.
sesame seeds soaked overnight and dehydrated until dry (optional)

Dressing
2 dessertspoons olive oil
½ teaspoon toasted sesame oil (optional)
1 teaspoon lemon juice
¼ teaspoon sea salt

Wash spinach leaves, drain well and place in serving bowl.
Blend all ingredients for the dressing together.
Toss dressing over spinach leaves.
Garnish with sesame seeds (optional).
Serve at once.

Preparation time: 10 minutes.

* page 58

Green Simplicity Salad

Spinach Salad

47

Two quick salads with a difference.

TOMATO, CUCUMBER & ONION SALAD

3 or 4 tomatoes
½ red onion
1 cucumber
basil

Marinade
2 dessertspoons apple cider vinegar*/lemon juice
4 dessertspoons cold pressed olive oil
½ teaspoon salt or to taste

Cube tomatoes and cucumber. Chop onion finely.
Layer in a dish tomato, cucumber and onion.
Blend all the ingredients for the marinade.
Pour marinade over the salad and let it stand for 30 minutes.
Sprinkle with basil just before serving.

Preparation time: 10 minutes.

* page 124

MEDITERRANEAN SALAD

2 red peppers and 2 yellow peppers
½ red onion
rocket
2 sticks celery

Marinade
2 dessertspoons apple cider vinegar*/lemon juice
4 dessertspoons cold pressed olive oil
½ teaspoon salt or to taste
1 clove garlic minced

Wash and deseed the peppers. Slice thinly.
Chop celery finely.
Slice red onion in circles.
Toss the vegetables with the rocket.
Blend all the ingredients for the marinade. Pour marinade over the salad and let it stand for at least 30 minutes. Serve.

Preparation time: 10 minutes.

I bought a lot of seaweed from Quality Sea Veg in Donegal without really knowing what to do with it, until one day I had two Japanese customers, Maki Mutai and Shobana Dheepson. The upshot of that conversation is the following recipe. Thank you girls!

JAPANESE SEA SALAD

25 g / 1 oz wakame* soaked in lukewarm water
for 10 to 15 minutes and drained
3 scallions diced
1 cucumber thinly sliced

Dressing
3 dessertspoons cold pressed olive oil
1 dessertspoon toasted sesame oil (optional)
2 dessertspoons lemon/lime juice
1 dessertspoon tamari**
1 dessertspoon grated ginger

Pat dry the soaked wakame* and dice.
Slice the cucumber.
Dice all the scallions.
Add the vegetables to the seaweed.
Make the dressing and pour over salad.
Allow to marinate for 30 minutes.
Serve.

Preparation time: 30 minutes.

salads

salads

salads

*Coleslaw is a welcome salad at any celebration.
This vegan one is a delight.*

COLESLAW

¼ head white cabbage
2 medium carrots
¼ red onion

Peel and trim the carrots.
Prepare cabbage and onion.
Shred the carrots and white cabbage finely.
Slice onion finely.
Mix with nut 'mayo'* and serve.
Use same day.

Preparation time: 20 minutes.

salads

RICH CHINESE SAUCE

zest of two oranges
4 dessertspoons lemon juice
75 ml / 3 fl. oz olive oil
75 ml / 3 fl. oz sunflower oil
2 dessertspoons toasted sesame oil
2 dessertspoons tamari*
½ teaspoon salt
½ teaspoon cayenne pepper
3 cloves garlic minced
3 dessertspoons grated ginger

Blend all the ingredients together in a blender.
Allow to stand for 30 minutes for flavours to blend.
Serve with sprouted quinoa or vegetables.**

Preparation time: 15 minutes.

sauces & dressings

sauces & dressings

sauces & dressings

These pickled vegetable recipes were invented by Kevin as accompaniments to the wraps. They make the wrap taste delicious and are also great with burgers.

`PICKLED` ONIONS
1 kg / 2.2 lb onions

Chop onions very finely and steep overnight in cold water. Strain next day.
Put onions into muslin cloth and squeeze out all the juice. Set aside.

Marinade
150 ml / ¼ pint of oil - any cold pressed oil
150 ml / ¼ pint apple cider vinegar*/lemon juice
4 dessertspoons honey/agave** syrup
1 teaspoon curry powder

Blend marinade together and pour over onions. Allow the onions to marinate for a few hours. Keeps for two weeks in a jar in the fridge.

Preparation time: 45 minutes.

'PICKLED` BEETROOT
200 g / 8 oz beetroot (peeled)

Marinade
2 dessertspoons organic honey/agave** syrup
2 dessertspoons apple cider vinegar*/lemon juice

In food processor, using the grater, grate the beetroot finely.
Blend marinade together and pour over beetroot.
Allow the beetroot to marinate for a few hours.
Keeps for one week in a jar in the fridge.

sauces & dressings

Preparation time: 25 minutes.

* page 124, ** page 124

I like using the pickled onion and cucumber for my burger! Awesome!

`PICKLED` CUCUMBER

2 cucumbers

Marinade
150 ml / ¼ pint filtered water
150 ml / ¼ pint apple cider vinegar*/lemon juice
75 ml / 3 fl. oz honey/agave syrup**

Peel cucumber and cut into very thin slices.
Blend marinade together and pour over cucumber.
Allow the cucumber to marinate for a few hours.
Will keep for one to two weeks in a jar in the fridge.

Preparation time: 15 minutes.

* page 124, ** page 124

NUT 'MAYO'

100 g / 4 oz almonds/cashews
(soak overnight, rinse and drain)
75 ml / 3 fl. oz cold pressed olive oil
50 ml / 2 fl. oz filtered water
½ teaspoon mustard powder
3 dessertspoons lemon juice
Place all ingredients into a blender and blend.

Serve as mayonnaise on your favourite salad.
Will last up to 3 days in the fridge.

Note: Skin the almonds using a little warm water.

Preparation time: 15 minutes.

FRENCH DRESSING

300 ml / ½ pint cold pressed olive oil
300 ml / ½ pint cold pressed sunflower oil
4 dessertspoons apple cider vinegar* or lemon juice
1 dessertspoon honey (if you want it sweeter,
add 2 dessertspoons)
3 dessertspoons mustard seeds
2 cloves garlic
sea salt to taste.

Place all ingredients in a blender and blend.
Serve as dressing to any salad. Store in fridge.
This dressing keeps for up to two weeks.

French Dressing

sauces & dressings

Preparation time: 15 minutes.

* page 124

If you are craving something a little spicy, these dressings are just the thing.

MILD CHILLI DRESSING

1 red bell pepper
1 mild chilli pepper
300 ml / ½ pint cold pressed olive oil
3 dessertspoons lemon juice
2 dessertspoons agave* syrup
pinch of cayenne pepper
salt to taste

Wash and deseed the bell pepper.
Using plastic gloves, wash and deseed the chilli pepper.
Place all ingredients in a blender and blend until smooth.
Taste and enjoy. Refrigerate and use within 3 - 4 days.

Preparation time: 15 minutes.

RICH TOMATO SAUCE

50 g / 2 oz dates soaked for two hours
100 g / 4 oz sundried tomatoes soaked for two hours
2 tomatoes deseeded
½ teaspoon chilli powder
1 teaspoon apple cider vinegar**/lemon juice
¼ teaspoon cayenne pepper

Using some of the date soak-water, blend the softened dates with the sundried tomatoes.
Add the rest of the ingredients. Allow to stand for flavours to blend.
Refrigerate and use within 3 days.
Use as Tomato Ketchup.

sauces & dressings

Preparation time: 15 minutes.

* page 124, ** page 124

Mild Chilli Dressing

sauces & dressings

Kevin experimented until he was satisfied with this 'mayo'.
It's a treat. Lovely in the wraps or as a spread or dip.

PUMPKIN SEED 'MAYO'

100 g / 4 oz pumpkin seeds soaked overnight
150 ml / ¼ pint sunflower or olive oil (cold pressed)
1 teaspoon sea salt or to taste
1 teaspoon onion powder
2 dessertspoons apple cider vinegar*/lemon juice
1 clove garlic
1 teaspoon curry
¼ teaspoon turmeric

Drain soaked pumpkin seeds. In a food processor, using the 'dough' or 4-spiked blade, rub the green coating from the pumpkin seeds.
Cover with water and allow the green scum to rise to surface.
Drain away. Repeat till pumpkin seeds are yellow in colour.
Drain.

This process is not essential - the pumpkin seeds may be used as they are. The 'mayo' will then be <u>green</u> in colour.

Blend the seeds with the rest of the ingredients in a blender until smooth and creamy.

Refrigerate. Keeps for two weeks in the fridge.

sauces & dressings

Preparation time: 60 minutes.

* page 124

I like this recipe for special occasions as it has a 'meaty' look and taste to it. Great for a party.

STUFFED PEPPERS

2 red peppers
2 yellow peppers

Clean the peppers. Cut off the tops. Remove seeds and rinse. Pat dry with a paper towel.
Place the peppers in a marinade of a little olive oil and lemon juice.

STUFFING

100 g / 4 oz walnuts soaked, rinsed and drained
100 g / 4 oz cashews/almonds soaked, rinsed and drained
50 g / 2 oz pine nuts soaked, rinsed and drained
1 dessertspoon white miso* (shiro)
bunch of fresh coriander/basil
½ teaspoon dried cumin
½ teaspoon dried oregano
sea salt to taste
1 scallion
1 dessertspoon corn (fresh or frozen)
1 diced medium tomato
1 teaspoon lime/lemon juice

In a food processor grind the nuts together.
Add the rest of the ingredients. Mix well.
Place stuffing in peppers and dehydrate for 4 hours at 42°c/115°f.
Serve.

Preparation time: 45 minutes.

entrées

My sister worked in Hafners (a famous sausage shop in Henry Street). I invented this recipe in memory of the taste of those sausages!

TRADITIONAL BURGERS

100 g / 4 oz almonds soaked for 8 hours, rinsed and drained
100 g / 4 oz walnuts soaked for 8 hours, rinsed and drained
175 g grated carrot
100 g minced onion
50 g peeled diced courgette
25 g red pepper
1 dessertspoon lemon juice
2 dessertspoons olive oil
1 dessertspoon mixed herbs
1 teaspoon thyme
1¼ teaspoons allspice
1 teaspoon nutmeg
½ teaspoon salt
½ teaspoon cayenne pepper

In a food processor, using the 'S' blade, grind nuts and leave aside.
Grate the carrots.
Chop the rest of the vegetables.
Place the vegetables in the food processor and, using the 'S' blade, process while adding nuts and seasonings.
Turn out onto board and form into burger patties.
Place on teflex* sheet or parchment.
Dehydrate for 4 - 6 hours, until firm.
Turn over half-way through and continue to dehydrate for 2 more hours.

Makes 12 burgers.
Preparation time: 45 minutes.

After trying many times, I finally came up with this Live Pizza. It's everyone's favourite.

LIVE PIZZA - *BASE, CASHEW CREAM SAUCE, PASTA SAUCE & TOPPINGS*

BASE

150 g / 6 oz courgettes peeled
150 g / 6 oz buckwheat* soaked for 15 minutes. Rinse (4 or 5 times)
150 g / 6 oz flaxmeal**
2 dessertspoons olive oil
2 teaspoons dried basil
1 teaspoon dried oregano
½ teaspoon salt
1 teaspoon onion powder
¼ teaspoon cayenne pepper

In a food processor, using the 'S' blade, process the peeled courgettes. Then add rinsed buckwheat and process.
Mix basil, oregano, salt, onion powder and cayenne pepper with the oil, and add to mixture in food processor.
Blend the flaxmeal** into the mixture. Mix well.
Roll onto a non-stick drying sheet, covering with a freezer bag to prevent mixture sticking to rolling pin.
Roll to size of sheet (5 mm thickness).
Remove covering from mixture, trim and cut to desired sizes.
Place on teflex*** sheets and dehydrate for 4 hours at 42°c/115°f.
Turn and continue to dehydrate for 2 more hours.
The pizza bases may be frozen and used as needed.
When serving, spread Pasta Sauce****, Cashew Cream Sauce***** and Toppings****** and dehydrate for ½ to 1 hour.

Yummy!

Preparation time: 45 minutes.

entrées

On the pizza base spread the Pasta Sauce first, then the Cashew Cream Sauce and finally add the Toppings.
(If you prefer, you can substitute almonds for cashews.)

CASHEW CREAM SAUCE

100 g / 4 oz cashews (or almonds) soaked overnight, rinsed and drained.
Discard water.
125 ml / approx. 4 fl. oz filtered water
2 dessertspoons cold pressed olive oil
dash of tamari*
2 teaspoons lemon juice
2 dessertspoons nutritional yeast flakes**
1 dessertspoon white miso*** (shiro)
pinch of salt

Pour the oil, filtered water and nuts into a blender. Blend.
(Rest the machine halfway through, if you need to.)
Add rest of ingredients. Blend till smooth, adding water if needed.
Place in a bowl and leave for 20 minutes.
This allows the sauce to thicken.

Preparation time: 25 minutes.

PASTA SAUCE

100 g / 4 oz sundried tomatoes soaked in filtered water
(approx. 2 hours)
100 g / 4 oz tomatoes chopped
100 g / 4 oz red peppers chopped
1 clove garlic
2 teaspoons dried basil
1 teaspoon dried oregano
pinch dried thyme
pinch cayenne pepper
½ apple chopped (optional)

Chop and place sundried tomatoes in blender with some
of the soak-water and blend.
Add rest of ingredients.
Depending on what consistency you want, add rest of soak-water.
Blend and place in a bowl, ready to use.

Preparation time: 20 minutes.

You can use all of these toppings for your pizza or just some of them. A few basil leaves adds a lovely finishing touch.

TOPPINGS FOR PIZZA

MUSHROOM MARINADE
100 g / 4 oz mushrooms
3 dessertspoons olive oil
1½ dessertspoons tamari*

Mix marinade and pour over sliced mushrooms.
Allow to marinate for 2 hours, drain and dehydrate for 2 hours.
May be used as a topping for pizza or wraps.

RED & YELLOW PEPPERS
Wash and cut into thin slices or dice.

RED ONION RINGS
Peel and cut into rings.

SUNDRIED TOMATOES & OLIVES
50 g / 2 oz sundried tomatoes, soaked
25 g / 1 oz stoned olives
1 dessertspoon olive oil
a little chopped onion

Strain the sundried tomatoes.
Dice and add chopped olives, olive oil and onion.

Preparation time: 25 minutes.

entrées

Mary O'Reilly, An Tairseach Organic Farm, Wicklow

This fun dish is great for all the family.

KEBABS

mushrooms
courgettes
onions or leeks
red peppers, yellow peppers
tomatoes

Marinade
150 ml / ¼ pint cold pressed olive oil
75 ml / 3 fl. oz tamari*

Wash and trim vegetables. Cut into bite-size pieces.
Mix marinade and pour over vegetables.
Marinate mushrooms separately.
Allow all to marinate for 2 hours, drain and place on skewers.
Dehydrate for 2 hours and serve.

Suggestion:
Cover kebabs with rich tomato sauce** and dehydrate
for 30 minutes.

Preparation time: 25 minutes.

entrées

This dish looks amazing. The colours are vibrant and inviting. Enjoy!

PASTA SURPRISE (Serves 4 - 6)

1 - 2 butternut squash*
2 - 3 courgettes
1 red pepper cut into thin strips
1 yellow pepper cut into thin strips
1 orange pepper cut into thin strips (optional)
1 red onion diced
bunch fresh parsley or basil

Marinade/Dressing
3 dessertspoons lemon juice
3 dessertspoons olive oil
2 dessertspoons garlic
2 dessertspoons oregano
1 teaspoon basil
1½ teaspoons cayenne pepper or to taste
1½ teaspoons sea salt

Peel butternut squash* and courgettes.
Using a spiralizer**, form butternut squash* and courgettes into pasta. If you do not have a spiralizer**, slice the butternut squash* and courgettes lengthways, then slice into long threads to resemble pasta.
Place in bowl and add the remaining ingredients.
Toss well and add the dressing.
Leave to marinate for 1 hour and serve.

Preparation time: 35 minutes.

entrées

These croquettes are very attractive and inviting.
I like making them for big groups.

ITALIAN CROQUETTES

200 g / 8 oz brazil nuts soaked overnight, then drained
50 g / 2 oz pine nuts soaked for 2 hours, then drained
2 dessertspoons lemon juice
3 stalks celery chopped
½ red onion chopped
2 medium tomatoes diced
¼ teaspoon cayenne pepper
2 cloves garlic minced
2 teaspoons dried basil
1 teaspoon dried oregano
½ yellow pepper diced
½ red pepper diced
bunch fresh parsley
1 teaspoon sea salt or to taste

Process the nuts in a food processor using the 'S' blade.
Leave aside.
Process all the vegetables in the food processor using the 'S' blade.
Add all the herbs and spices. Blend well.
Add the ground nuts. Mix.
(If the amount is too much for the processor, do it in two batches.)
Form into croquettes about 50 mm (2 inches) in diameter.
Place on teflex* sheet or parchment.
Dehydrate at 42°c/115°f for 4 - 6 hours or until firm.
Turn over half-way through and continue to dehydrate for
1 - 2 more hours.
Note: They may also be served without dehydrating.
Delicious.

Preparation time: 35 minutes.

entrées

This dish is full of goodness, and mild in flavour.

QUINOA*   (Serves 4 - 6)

200 g / 8 oz of quinoa*
1 avocado
1 red pepper
1 yellow pepper
4 scallions
basil for garnish

Dressing
4 dessertspoons cold pressed sunflower oil/olive oil
1 dessertspoon honey/agave** syrup (optional)
dash cayenne pepper
1 dessertspoon lemon juice
salt to taste

How to sprout quinoa:*
Soak the quinoa* in filtered water overnight.
Rinse next morning and drain.

Place the drained, sprouted quinoa* in a bowl.
Dice the avocado and the peppers and add to quinoa*.
Chop the scallions finely and add.
Chop basil and add.
Blend the ingredients for the dressing and pour over the quinoa*.
Mix well and allow to stand for at least 30 minutes.
Serve.

Preparation time: 35 minutes.

entrées

If you like something a little different, try these.

ASIAN CROQUETTES

200 g / 8 oz brazil nuts soaked overnight and drained
50 g / 2 oz pine nuts soaked overnight and drained
3 portobello mushrooms marinated for 2 hours
(*Marinade*: 1 dessertspoon tamari* + 2 dessertspoons olive oil)
2 dessertspoons lemon juice
½ teaspoon cayenne pepper
½ red onion chopped
3 stalks celery
2 medium tomatoes diced
2 cloves garlic minced
1 teaspoon grated ginger
1 teaspoon mixed herbs
bunch fresh parsley
1 teaspoon sea salt or to taste

Process the nuts in a food processor using the 'S' blade.
Leave aside.
Process all the vegetables in the food processor using the 'S' blade.
Add all the herbs and spices. Blend well.
Add the ground nuts. Mix.
(If the amount is too much for the processor, do it in two batches.)
Form into croquettes about 50 mm (2 inches) in diameter.
Place on teflex** sheet or parchment.
Dehydrate at 42°c/115°f for 4 - 6 hours until firm.
Turn over half-way through and continue to dehydrate for
1 - 2 more hours.
Note: They may also be served without dehydrating.
Delicious.

Preparation time: 35 minutes.

entrées

* page 127, ** page 120

This dish is ideal for those winter months when you are craving something warm and comforting.

STIR RAW

100 g / 4 oz mushrooms sliced
2 yellow bell peppers julienned*
broccoli florets
a little red cabbage shredded
1 red onion cut into thin rings
fresh herbs

Marinade
4 dessertspoons olive oil
2 dessertspoons tamari**
2 dessertspoons lemon juice
½ teaspoon grated fresh ginger
1 clove garlic minced

Blend all the ingredients for the marinade and allow to marinate for 1 hour.
Prepare the vegetables.
Pour marinade over the vegetables.
Allow to sit for at least 30 minutes.
Dehydrate for about 1 hour or longer before serving.
Garnish with fresh herbs.

Preparation time: 25 minutes.

One night, I was too tired to use up already soaked nuts for a 'cheese' cake, so I decided to mix them together with some seasonings and dehydrate overnight. This was the result. It went down a treat.

NUT CRUNCH

150 g / 6 oz cashews soaked overnight, rinsed and drained
50 g / 2 oz walnuts soaked overnight and drained
50 g / 2 oz brazil nuts soaked overnight and drained
2 dessertspoons tamari*
1 teaspoon curry powder
2 level teaspoons chilli powder (mild)

Using the 'S' blade, process the nuts in a food processor (until they look like breadcrumbs).
Place in a bowl and mix in the seasonings. Taste.
Spread onto teflex** sheet and dehydrate for 6 hours.
Turn over half-way through and continue to dehydrate for 3 more hours.

Keeps for one month in an airtight container.

Preparation time: 15 minutes.

* page 127, ** page 120

This is a filling dish. Lovely for winter days.

BARLEY PILAF

300 g / 12 oz of barley (pot barley) soaked for 24 hours
1 medium red pepper diced
1 medium yellow pepper diced
4 scallions chopped finely

Dressing
4 dessertspoons cold pressed olive oil
2 dessertspoons tamari*
2 dessertspoons chopped parsley

Drain barley and add all the diced vegetables.
Mix dressing and pour over barley.
Allow to stand for 30 minutes.
Serve.

Preparation time: 15 minutes.

entrées

'RICE'

50 g / 2 oz pine nuts soaked for 3 hours, then drained
1 parsnip
½ head of cauliflower
1 bunch fresh coriander chopped
¼ red onion diced
1 teaspoon salt
2 dessertspoons olive oil
1 teaspoon onion powder (optional)

Peel parsnip and chop cauliflower.
Process in a food processor using the 'S' blade.
Add the pine nuts and pulse until a rice-like consistency is obtained.
Place in a bowl and add the diced onion and chopped coriander.
Add the rest of the ingredients.
Serve.

Nori Rolls

Preparation time: 15 minutes.

entrées

Rice Mound

Gabrielle Kirby suggested I try and make Ice Cream out of avocado. After experimenting for a while, this is what I came up with. It 's really lovely, even for the person who doesn't like avocado!

PEPPERMINT 'ICE CREAM'   (Serves 2)

1 avocado
150 ml / ¼ pint coconut milk*
1½ teaspoons peppermint essence (or to taste)
2 dessertspoons expeller pressed coconut oil** (to melt, place container in bowl of warm water)
1 teaspoon lime juice
3 dessertspoons agave*** syrup

Blend all the ingredients and pour into Ice Cream Maker.
Follow the manufactures instructions.

If you don't have a Ice Cream Maker, freeze in a bowl for 2 hours.
Take out.
Remix and freeze again.

'Chocolate' Sauce Topping
2 dessertspoons agave*** syrup
1 dessertspoon Green & Black's cocoa powder****

Mix ingredients.

Pour 'Chocolate' Sauce over 'Ice Cream'.
Serve.

Preparation time: 25 minutes.

This refreshing fruit salad is very quick to make.
Ideal for those busy moments.

BERRY FRUIT SALAD

50 g / 2 oz strawberries
50 g / 2 oz blackberries
50 g / 2 oz raspberries
a little chopped mint

Syrup
1 dessertspoon filtered water
½ teaspoon lemon juice
1 teaspoon agave* syrup

Wash and dehull the berries.
Leave aside.
Blend the filtered water, lemon juice and agave* together.
Pour over fruit and mix.
Allow to stand for thirty minutes.
Add chopped mint.
Serve with your favourite sauce or coconut cream**.

Preparation time: 15 minutes.

desserts

* page 124, ** page 102

*'Cheese' Cake is a tasty treat for that special occasion.
Very popular with everyone.*

BERRY `CHEESE` CAKE - *BASE, FILLING & TOPPING*

BASE
100 g / 4 oz walnuts (soak for 8 hours or overnight, drain)
100 g / 4 oz brazil nuts soaked overnight and drained
4 dates soaked for 2 hours approx. (Reserve the soak-water.)
dash of nutmeg

Process nuts, dates and seasonings in food processor until dough.
Press mixture into a spring-form cake tin (23 cm/9 in) to form
a base.

FILLING
300 g / 12 oz cashew nuts (soaked for 8 hours or overnight)
150 ml / ¼ pint honey/agave* syrup
1½ dessertspoons psyllium husks**
1½ dessertspoons lecithin granules***
juice of 1 lemon
1 vanilla pod or 1 teaspoon vanilla essence
150 ml / ¼ pint filtered water (or use the date soak-water)
50 g / 2 oz berries (may be frozen, but allow to thaw first)
½ teaspoon salt
150 ml / ¼ pint coconut oil (to melt, place container in
bowl of warm water)

Put the liquid into the blender and add all the ingredients. Blend.

Variations (instead of using berries for filling)
'Choc Cheese' Cake - 1 cup Green & Black's cocoa powder****
Lemon or Lime 'Cheese' Cake - zest of 2 lemons or 2 limes

TOPPING
Fruit, flower, leaf, or sauce of your choice

Preparation time: 25 minutes.

* page 124, ** page 126, *** page 126, **** page 125   92

Strawberry 'Cheese' Cake

'Choc Cheese' Cake

Lime 'Cheese' Cake

Lemon 'Cheese' Cake

These treats are great for parties and also are lovely gifts for your friends.

'CHOC` TRUFFLES

100 g / 4 oz almonds (or any nuts) soaked overnight, drained
50 g / 2 oz sunflower seeds soaked overnight, drained
2 dessertspoons agave* syrup or honey
4 dessertspoons cocoa powder (Green & Black's**)
few drops of vanilla essence
few drops of rum essence
desiccated coconut for decoration

In food processor finely chop nuts and sunflower seeds.
Add all the other ingredients.
Mix well.
Form into small balls. Chill and serve.

Preparation time: 25 minutes.

These bars are moist, with a lovely fruity taste.

SPICE BARS

150 g / 6 oz dried apricots (soaked for 1 hour)
150 g / 6 oz raisins
100 g / 4 oz almonds/cashews soaked overnight
100 g / 4 oz brazils soaked overnight
1 dessertspoon vanilla essence
zest of 2 oranges
1 dessertspoon mixed spice
¼ teaspoon ground cloves
1 teaspoon ground ginger
1 dessertspoon coconut oil (melt before using)

Drain the apricots. Rinse and drain the nuts.
Place all the ingredients in a food processor and, using the
'S' blade, process until the mixture forms a dough.
Place the mixture on a baking tray and press firmly to cover the
tray.
Score the size of bars you would like and place in the fridge
to set.
These bars resemble the texture of Christmas Pudding.
Lovely served with coconut cream*.

Preparation time: 45 minutes.

These bars are lovely at any time. Great for taking to work or for travelling. Experiment with your own favourite seasonings.

ENERGY BARS

100 g / 4 oz sunflower seeds soaked overnight and drained
200 g / 8 oz brazil nuts soaked overnight and drained
100 g / 4 oz dates soaked for 2 hours - retain the water
100 g / 4 oz raisins soaked for 2 hours - retain the water
½ teaspoon mixed spice
½ teaspoon ground ginger

Blend nuts and seeds in a food processor using the 'S' blade.
Chop dates and add to mixture. Pulse.
Add raisins and spices. Pulse.
Add some of the soak-water from the dates and raisins.
Blend.
Place mixture on a teflex* sheet and cover loosely with parchment
or a large freezer bag to prevent mixture sticking to rolling pin.
Roll to size of sheet (3mm thickness).
Remove the parchment/freezer bag.
Trim edges and, using a knife, score the mixture to mark out bars.
Place on dehydrator** shelf and dehydrate for 12 hours or
overnight at 42°c/115°f.
Turn and continue to dehydrate for 4 more hours.
Store in airtight container.
Will keep for a month or two.

Preparation time: 45 minutes.

Dehydrator**

This is lovely for a treat when you want something a little substantial as well as sweet.

SURPRISE MOUSSE

3 avocados
100 g / 4 oz Green & Black's organic cocoa powder*
50 g / 2 oz dates soaked for 2 hours in orange juice
5 dessertspoons agave** syrup
1 teaspoon tamari***
1 teaspoon cinnamon powder
1 vanilla pod or 1 teaspoon vanilla essence
zest of 2 oranges

Peel and pit the avocados.
Drain and chop the dates, retaining the soak-water.
In a food processor, using the 'S blade, blend the dates with a little of the soak-water.
Prepare the vanilla pod (or use vanilla essence) and add to the mix with all the other ingredients.
Blend until smooth.
(Note: if you wish, you can blend everything in a blender instead of a food processor. Blend until smooth, adding soak-water if needed.)
Chill for about 1 hour.
Serve with segments of orange and coconut cream****.

Preparation time: 35 minutes.

desserts

This recipe is one of Kevin's creations. We had great fun tasting it every day as he worked to perfect it. It 's a fantastic way to bring sea vegetables into the diet.

KEVIN'S COCONUT DREAM CAKE

50 g / 2 oz carragheen* (Irish Moss)
300 g / 12 oz desiccated coconut
150 ml / ¼ pint clear honey/agave** syrup
6 dessertspoons lecithin granules*** (non GMO)
juice of ½ lemon
zest of 1 lemon

Soak the carragheen* (Irish moss) overnight, then drain.
Discard soak-water and rinse well.
Put the carragheen* into a high-speed blender with
150 ml (¼ pint) of filtered water and blend.
Strain liquid though muslin/cheese cloth. Discard pulp.
Set the carragheen* aside.

Soak the coconut with 900 ml (1½ pints) of warm water for a few minutes. Then blend.
Strain through muslin/cheese cloth.
Use milk only for the cake. (Pulp may be used for making crackers.)

In blender, add the carragheen*, coconut milk and the rest of the ingredients. Blend.
Pour into a mould, or line a spring-form cake tin with cling film and pour mixture into it.
Allow to set in a refrigerator for a minimum of 4 hours.
Decorate and serve.

Note: If making a chocolate-flavoured cake,
add 1 cup of Green & Black's cocoa powder****.

Preparation time: 35 minutes.

* page 124, ** page 124, *** page 126, **** page 125

These two recipes were created by Kevin. The milk is quite sweet and it's great to try the cream on your favourite dessert. Yummy!!!

COCONUT MILK

150 g / 6 oz desiccated coconut
1 litre / 1¾ pints warm filtered water

Put the coconut into a blender with half the filtered water and blend until it becomes a smooth cream. Add the rest of the filtered water.
When the coconut is finally blended, strain through a bag (cheese cloth/muslin/nut milk bag).
The pulp will remain in the bag and may be used for biscuits etc. Serve.
Note: Stir the milk at regular intervals.

Preparation time: 10 minutes.

COCONUT CREAM

Coconut Milk (approx. 2 litres) - see recipe above

Do not stir.
Place in the fridge and do not disturb for 8 hours.
Milk must settle to form a solid block with all the water underneath it. (Water may be used for smoothies.)
Cut two small holes in block and drain water.
Break the block into small pieces and stir/whisk or whip with an electric beater until creamy.
Add agave* syrup/honey and flavouring of your choice.
Serve over dessert.

Preparation time: 10 minutes.

beverages

I made this recipe originally for the 'Alive' (Irish Living Food Association) Christmas Party. It's very warming and festive.

FRUITY PUNCH   (Serves 6 - 8)

1 litre / 1¾ pints apple juice
½ litre / 1 pint approx. orange juice
2 dessertspoons lemon juice
1 dessertspoon lime juice
125 g / 5 oz raisins
25 g / 1 oz mulling spices*
Fruit of your choice

Pour the apple, orange, lime and lemon juices into a saucepan. Add raisins.
Place the mulling spices into a muslin cloth and tie with string.
Simmer to a temperature of 42°c/115°f, or a little less, for about 2 hours.
Add bite-size pieces of fruit of your choice - orange, apple, pear, etc.
Taste and adjust flavouring (may need a little honey, depending on the tartness of the fruit).
Remove mulling spices.
Serve in warm glasses.

Preparation time: 40 minutes.

beverages

beverages

beverages

Gabrielle gave me this recipe. It's a great alternative to a nut milk, brilliant for smoothies and full of absorbable calcium.

SESAME SEED MILK

100 g / 4 oz sesame seeds soaked overnight
1½ litres / 2½ pints filtered water

Strain seeds.
Blend the seeds, with some of the filtered water, in a blender for a few minutes. Add the rest of the water.
Strain through a nut bag or muslin cloth, and you have delicious milk.
(The pulp may be used in other dishes or dehydrated and ground to make flour.)
Refrigerate.
Keeps for three days.

Preparation time: 10 minutes.

ALMOND MILK (for a special treat)

100 g / 4 oz almonds soaked overnight
1½ litres / 2½ pints filtered water
1 vanilla pod or 1 teaspoon vanilla essence
4 teaspoons honey/agave* syrup

Drain and skin the soaked nuts.
Blend the nuts with the filtered water.
Strain through a nut bag or muslin cloth.
(The pulp may be used in other dishes or dehydrated and ground to make almond flour.)
Prepare the vanilla pod (or use vanilla essence) and add to the milk with honey or agave* syrup.
Blend and serve.

Preparation time: 10 minutes.

* page 124

Sesame Milk

Smoothies are a great treat at any time. They're very popular with children. I love Mango Madness.

GREEN SMOOTHIE SURPRISE   (Serves 1)

2 bananas
handful of spinach
150 ml / ¼ pint almond*/coconut**/sesame milk***

Pour milk into blender and add bananas. Blend.
Add the spinach. Blend & serve.

Preparation time: 5 minutes.

MINTY SMOOTHIE   (Serves 1)

2 bananas
1 kiwi
150 ml / ¼ pint almond*/coconut**/sesame milk***
a few leaves of mint

Pour milk into blender. Add bananas, peeled kiwi and mint. Blend and serve.

Preparation time: 5 minutes.

MANGO MADNESS

150 ml / ¼ pint fresh orange juice
 2 bananas
3 dessertspoons mango

Pour orange juice into blender.
Add bananas and mango. Blend and serve.

Preparation time: 10 minutes.

* page 106, ** page 102, *** page 106

I like using frozen berries for this one, when I can't get fresh ones.

BERRY SMOOTHIE   (Serves 1 - 2)

2 bananas
50 g / 2 oz fresh blackberries
150 ml / ¼ pint almond*/coconut/sesame milk*****

Pour milk into blender.
Add bananas and cleaned berries. Blend & serve.

Preparation time: 5 minutes.

Minty Smoothie

Berry Smoothie

Mango Madness

* page 106, ** page 102, *** page 106

These simple juices are very popular. Experiment to find your own favourite.

GINGERED CARROT

3 carrots
1 apple
1 stick of celery
ginger to taste

Wash, peel and prepare ingredients.
Juice and serve.

Preparation time: 8 minutes.

CLEAN GREEN

½ cucumber
1 apple
2 sticks of celery

Wash, peel and prepare ingredients.
Juice and serve.

Preparation time: 8 minutes.

TWISTER

2 apples
½ cucumber
juice of ¼ lemon

Wash, peel and prepare
ingredients.
Juice and serve.

Preparation time: 8 minutes.

beverages

A juice is lovely around mid-morning.

SPICEY DICEY

3 carrots
1 apple
1 leaf kale or cabbage
ginger to taste
pinch cayenne pepper

Wash, peel and prepare ingredients.
Juice and serve.

Preparation time: 8 minutes.

beverages

SWEET NECTAR

½ cucumber
1 apple
1 pear

Wash, peel and prepare ingredients.
Juice and serve.

Preparation time: 8 minutes.

Green smoothies are for extra energy and great to experiment with.

GREEN POWER

A little filtered water
2 sticks of celery chopped
½ cucumber chopped
1 apple sliced
small bunch spinach or any sprouts (pea greens, sunflower, etc.)

Optional Extras
Add all of these or try out one at a time...
1 slice ginger root (chopped finely)
½ clove garlic (skin may be left on)
pinch of cayenne
pinch of turmeric

Put the filtered water in a blender first, then add the rest of the ingredients.
Start on low for 20 seconds, then high for about 1 minute or until mix is well blended.
This blend is a great way to start the day and only takes minutes to prepare in a blender.

Preparation time: 5 minutes.

Sunflower Sprouts

beverages

Pea Green Sprouts

GREEN SMOOTHIE TIPS

Any of these may be added to smoothies for extra nutrition...

I teaspoon flax seeds
1 teaspoon pumpkin/sunflower seeds (soak overnight, drain, discard water)
1 teaspoon cold pressed seed oils
¼ teaspoon grated ginger
1 teaspoon tahini**
1 teaspoon lecithin granules***

New Beginnings:

After years of eating cooked food, it takes a mind-shift to consider eating raw vegan/vegetarian food. But the idea behind raw food is to eat for the optimum health benefit to our lives. It does not mean everyone has to 'Go Raw' or to be 80%, 90% or 100% 'Raw'.

All of us eat 'Raw' food already - all sorts of fruits and salads - without thinking about it. This book just extends the possibilities - soups, entrées and desserts. You may love white bread, so try brown bread instead, or bread with ingredients that are more organic. If you like chocolate, make a batch of 'Choc' Truffles* to have in the cupboard for those tempting moments.

Here are some more simple suggestions to help change our eating habits...

Make one little change that you are happy with, say one a month, and let it become the norm before you go further. Food is an important part of our lives. Making it tasty and presenting it beautifully will be well worth the effort.

Prepare food with love. If you are not in a loving mood, take a break and either allow someone else to prepare the food or wait till you feel you are able to do it with love. It does make a difference. I know one chef who will not allow himself or others to touch the food until it can be done with love.

Chew food thoroughly. This helps break it down and makes it easier to digest.

Be open to inspiration. I love looking at all types of cookery programmes. I learn something new from each one. Read cookery books and Raw Food Preparation books. Exchange ideas with like-minded people. Have fun!

Change yourself gradually, and allow others to make their own changes in their own time.

Enjoy the journey.

Cupboard Stores

Beans

aduki beans
lentils
mung beans

Nuts

almond
brazil
cashew
hazelnut
pecans
pistachio
walnut

Spices

allspice
cinnamon
cayenne pepper
cloves
cumin
curry powder
garlic powder
garlic granules
ginger
ground mustard
nutmeg
mild chilli
mixed spice
onion powder
paprika
turmeric

Fresh Spices

garlic
ginger
lemongrass

Sprouts

alfalfa
baby pea greens
broccoli
fenugreek
garlic chives
radish
red clover
sunflower greens

Dried/Fresh Herbs

basil
chives
coriander
dill
oregano
mint
parsley
rosemary
thyme
sage

Dried Fruit

apricots
dates
figs
raisins
prunes

Seeds

hemp
mustard seeds
poppy seeds
pumpkin
sesame
sunflower

Oil

coconut oil
olive oil
sunflower oil

Miscellaneous

chocolate extract
desiccated coconut
dulse flakes
Green & Black's cocoa powder
lecithin granules (GMO free)
nutritional yeast flakes
organic vanilla extract
peppermint extract
rum essence
sea salt
tamari
vanilla pod

Sprouting Guidelines

Seeds:

Soak overnight. Use a jar with a wide neck and with a screen of muslin, net, etc.

Generally add 4 times the volume of water to seeds.

Drain well, placing the jar at an angle of 45 degrees (a draining board is ideal).

Rinse morning and evening.

When the seeds begin to sprout, leave them in sunlight (though not direct sunlight) to form little green leaves.

Eat when ready – can be stored in the refrigerator for awhile in a sealed container.

Important to check smell and look. Discard if any of the following occur.

> Bad odour
> Soft or soggy spots
> Darkening of roots
> Leaves darkening or losing colour

Sprouts are low-cost, high-quality nutrients and can be used in salads and wraps.

Beans:

Soak overnight. Use a jar with a wide neck and with a screen of muslin, net, etc.

Generally add 4 times the volume of water to seeds (aduki and mung beans are best soaked in _warm water for 24 hours_ before draining).

Drain well, placing the jar at an angle of 45 degrees (a draining board is ideal).

Rinse morning and evening.

Beans are ready to eat when the little shoot is roughly the same size as the bean.

Eat when ready – can be stored in the refrigerator for a while (one week) in a sealed jar or container.

Check before serving that all beans are sprouted. Discard any that haven't.

Food Combining Tips

A lot has being written about food combining.
Here are some simple guidelines which may be helpful...
Eat proteins and vegetables together.
Eat carbohydrates and vegetables together.
Eat nuts and seeds together, but not with anything else.
Eat the same type of fruits together - acid with acid fruit, etc.
Eat melon on its own or with other types of melon.
Eat only one type of fat (oil or avocado) with vegetables.
Drink beverages 10 or 20 minutes before a meal or 2 - 3 hours afterwards.
Water may be sipped at a meal.

General:

Soak all seeds and nuts before using. This soaking removes the enzyme inhibitors and makes the seeds/nuts easier to digest.
Exceptions are brazils and hazelnuts, which don't require soaking. However, soaking softens these nuts making them easier on blenders, etc.
Soak at room temperature for 8 - 10 hours or overnight. Drain.

Note: If you have a dehydrator*, you can dehydrate the drained nuts and seeds and store in sealed containers until you need them.

Raw food takes planning.

Prepare for the week, not forgetting to use leftovers.

Whenever possible, buy seasonal vegetables.

Buy in bulk whenever possible, particularly nuts and seeds.

Compost whatever you can. If you don't have somewhere to compost, perhaps a neighbour can use your compost material.

Buy organic whenever you can, but don't worry if you can't get organic.

* page 120   117

Health & Safety

Purchase goods from reputable suppliers.

Zone your shopping bags - one for fruits and vegetables, and one for cleaning -sprays/washing-up liquid, etc.

Store in a suitable place. A cool, dry, dust-free, shaded place is best.

Always wash vegetables thoroughly, particularly organic vegetables. A little white vinegar in the water helps.

Wash chopping board and knives after each preparation.

Put away leftovers in sealed containers, or freeze, marking everything clearly.

Wash knives on their own, never leave at the bottom of a washing basin.

Carry knives by your side, point facing down to prevent accidents.

Sharpen knives regularly.

Rotate food so that the oldest is used first.

Check dates as regards dry ingredients and only buy enough to use in the stated time frame.

Read the manuals for your machines - food processor, blender, etc. and follow manufacturer's instructions.

Keep a First Aid Kit. Check it is stocked regularly.
Ensure awareness of where it is located and, when used, always leave it back in the same place.

Ensure smoke alarms are in working order.

A fire drill is good safety practice.

Guidelines for Food Preparation

1. **Delivery**
2. **Storage**
3. **Preparation**
4. **Serving**
5. **Leftovers**
6. **Cleaning**

Washing hands often is the simplest and easiest way to ensure a healthy kitchen.
Examine your pest control (flies, insects, rodents, etc.) regularly and update when necessary.

1. Delivery/Shopping
   Store frozen food as soon as possible in the freezer or, if using soon, allow to defrost in a fridge, making sure it doesn't drain onto the next shelf.
   Check all your products and store appropriately.

2. Storage in a Refrigerator
   Keep the same items together.
   Raw vegetables and fruit at the bottom of the fridge.
   Prepared foods on the middle shelf.
   Sensitive foods towards the top (nut milk, etc.).

3. Preparation
   Clean the preparation area including the sink.
   Use food-grade chopping boards. Clean between each use.
   Keep one board just for fruit and vegetables.

4. Check food is ready to serve.
   Check serving spoons, and serve with love.

5. Store leftovers in sealed containers in the fridge, dated with 'use by' date.

6. Wash all surfaces with soapy, hot water. Wipe down with 'Lilly's'*
   Spray Cleaner, or your favourite cleaner, sprayed onto a clean cloth.

Kitchen Tools

Here are some of the basic utensils that make preparing Living Food easy.

Blender:
A blender is ideal for making dressings, blends and sauces. Always read the instruction manual for your machine and follow the guidelines.
If possible get a strong blender, like a Vitamix.

Citrus Juicer:
This can be a simple hand-juicer or an electric one.

Food Dehydrator:
A dehydrator removes water from food. It enhances flavours and gives an appearance of 'cooked' without actually cooking. The temperature to dehydrate foods at is 115° Fahrenheit (or 42° Celsius) to preserve enzymes. You may start at 145° for the first hour and then lower it to 115°.

Food Processor:
Another great tool is the food processor. This machine comes with different blades which help chop, grind and mix. Again, always read the instruction manual for your machine and follow the guidelines.

Grinder:
Some food processors come with a small coffee grinder.
The grinder is used to grind small quantities of seeds, spices or nuts.

Juicer:
The best type of juicer is a masticating juicer. There are many on the market. Some, like the Green Star, come with a 'blank' which allows you to make desserts such as frozen banana 'ice cream'.

Spiralizer:
This is an optional tool. It makes courgette and butternut squash into pasta shapes.

Teflex:
Teflex sheets are non-stick sheets for use with a dehydrator. They are washable and re-useable.

Knives:

A chef knife (large knife)
A paring knife
A serrated knife
A palette knife

knife sharpener

Other:

cake tins
colander
cutting boards
funnels (all sizes)
grater
ladles
mixing bowls
measuring jug
mandolin
rolling pin
spatulas (all sizes)
sprout bag/nut milk bag
strainers (all sizes)
weighing scales

storage containers

Resources

Healthy Habits Cafe,
Quarantine Hill,
Wicklow Town,
Co. Wicklow
0404 68645
087 1469812
rawveronica@gmail.com
www.healthyhabs.com

Natasha's Living Foods,
www.natashaslivingfood.ie

Organic Vegetables:

An Tairseach,
Dominican Farm and Ecology Centre,
Wicklow Town,
Co. Wicklow
0404 61833/61914
www.ecocentrewicklow.ie

Sheane's Cottage Garden,
Ballinabarney,
Co. Wicklow
086 8809340

Dublin Food Co-Op,
12 Newmarket,
Dublin 6
01 4544258
www.dublinfood.coop

The Natural Food Market,
St. Andrews,
Pearse St.,
Dublin 2
01 6771930
www.supernatural.ie

The Happy Pear,
Church Rd,
Greystones,
Co. Wicklow
01 2873655
www.thehappypear.ie

Select Stores,
36 Tubbermore Rd.,
Dalkey,
Co. Dublin
01 2859611

Sea Vegetables:

Quality Sea Veg.,
Cloughglass,
Burtonport,
Co. Donegal
074 9542159

Organic Coconut Oil:

Tropical Oils Europe Ltd.
Kindlestown Hill,
Delgany
Co.Wicklow.
Ireland
Tel : +353 (0)404 62443
Web : www.tropicaloilseurope.com
E-mail : sales@tropicaloilseurope.

Natural Cleaning:

Lilly's Eco Clean Ltd.,
Unit 8,
Centra Commercial Park,
Castletownbere,
Co. Cork
027 71632
www.lillysecoluv.com

School

The Irish School of Herbal Medicine,
www.herbeire.ie

Vegetarian Restaurants:

Cornucopia,
19 - 20 Wicklow St.,
Dublin 2
01 677 7583
www.cornucopia.ie
(serves some living food dishes)

Juicers:

Bernard Kirby
0404 68645
www.healthyhabs.com

Raw Food Support Groups:

Alive - Irish Living Food Assoc.,
Quarantine Hill,
Wicklow Town,
Co. Wicklow
0404 68645
gabrielle@eircom.net
www.irishlivingfoods.com

Useful Websites:

www.healthyhabs.com
www.gabriellekirby.com
www.irishlivingfoods.com
www.theservanstsoflove.com
www.changesimply.com
www.hippocrates.inst.com
www.naturalusa.com/viktor
www.jillswyers.com
www.organicguide.ie

Glossary

Aduki Beans: A small red bean. Easy to sprout. Has a slightly nutty flavour.

Agave Syrup/Nectar: Sweetener that comes from a cactus-like plant grown in Mexico. It is sweeter than sugar and looks like a thinner version of maple syrup.

Almond Flour: This is the pulp left over from making almond milk. The pulp is dehydrated, ground and stored in an airtight container. It is used for adding to cheeses and biscuits.

Apple Cider Vinegar: A vinegar made from apples.

Avocado: Actually a fruit, though commonly regarded as a vegetable. It is used for salads and desserts.

Bragg Liquid Aminos: An alternative to salt. It is an unfermented soy sauce made from organic soybeans.

Buckwheat: Mild in flavour, though not a grain, is treated like one. Unhulled, it can be sprouted into 'baby greens'. The hulled buckwheat may be sprouted, dehydrated and used as a cereal or added to other dishes.

Butternut Squash: A winter squash with a sweet nutty flavour.

Carragheen/Irish Moss: This is a relatively small Red Algae seaweed, little more than 20 cm long. It has great thickening qualities.

Chickpea: Quite a large bean, brown-yellow in colour. It is sprouted and used in salads, or for making spreads such as hummus.

Chiffonnade: A way of chopping leafy vegetables. Roll the leaves into a cigar -type roll and cut into thin ribbons.

Chilli powder: A blend of spices including cumin, oregano, coriander, garlic, allspice, cloves and cayenne.

Creamed Coconut: Pure coconut, usually in white, solid block form, used for grating in many dishes, both savoury and sweet.

Coconut Oil or Butter: Unrefined coconut oil.

Courgette: A small cucumber-like squash. Usually used for pasta.

Crudités: Raw vegetables cut into thin strips.

Dehydrator: A machine or 'Raw Oven' used to dehydrate food. It preserves the food's enzymes, gives a 'cooked' appearance and concentrates flavour.

Dice: To cut fruit or vegetables into small cubes of 3 - 5 cm (¼ - ½ inch).

Drain: To strain liquid from a soaking food.

Dried Fruit: A fruit that has been dehydrated. It can be stored for long periods of time.

Dulse: A dark, purplish-red seaweed found on the North Atlantic Coastline. Plentiful off the west coast of Ireland.

Enzyme: Chemical protein complexes that promote body processes. There are more enzymes in raw food than cooked food.

Enzyme Inhibitors: Chemical protein complexes that hinder enzymes working. Soaking disables the inhibitors so the enzymes are released to do their job.

Expeller Pressed Coconut Oil: Has a neutral flavour (because it is semi-refined), yet it contains the same medium-chain fatty acids as coconut oil.

Fenugreek: A small yellowish-brown seed.

Flax: The small brown or golden seed of a perennial herb. It has a nutty flavour and also great gelatinous properties. Also known as 'linseed'.

Flaxmeal: Ground flax seeds.

Fennel Bulb: A white or pale-green bulb. Its aromatic taste is unique, strikingly reminiscent of licorice (liquorice) and aniseed.

Green & Black's Organic Cocoa Powder: Unsweetened cocoa powder.

Hemp Seed: A small seed which contains essential amino acids and fats.

Hulled/Hulling: The outer husk of a seed or grain is removed. The calyx of fruit, such as strawberry, is removed.

Juicer: A machine used to separate liquid from plants or fruit.

Julienne: Vegetables or fruit cut into fine, equal-length strips.

Kebabs: Skewered vegetables.

Kelp: A type of large, marine algae/seaweed.

Lecithin Granules: Made from pure, natural soya lecithin. Helps in the breakdown of fats.

Marinade: A flavoured liquid made by soaking food.

Marinate: To allow food to sit in a liquid mixture to soften and infuse flavour.

Miso (Shiro): A white (Shiro means 'white') miso, or traditional Japanese paste, made by fermenting soy beans and rice.

Mulling Spices: A collection of spices - allspice, nutmeg, cloves, cinnamon, star anise and various dried fruit peels in a cheese cloth bundle.

Mustard Powder: This powder is made from shelled mustard seeds.

Mustard Seeds: Small seeds of various mustard plants. Black, brown and yellow.

Mung Bean: A small, green bean.

Nori: Thin dried seaweed sheets.

Nutritional Yeast Flakes: Yeast (in form of flakes) grown for its nutritional benefits.

Onion Powder: Dehydrated onions ground into powder.

Oxidation: A reaction that occurs when food comes in contact with oxygen.

Paté: A smooth paste made from nuts or seeds, vegetables and seasonings.

Psyllium: A high fibre plant, the husks of which are used as a thickening agent in raw food.

Quinoa: This seed contains all nine essential amino acids, making it a complete vegetable protein.

'S' Blade: An 'S' shaped blade that comes as standard with a food processor.

Sesame Oil: A mild oil made from sesame seeds.

Shred: To cut vegetables using a hand-grater or the shredding attachment of a food processor.

Soak: To leave food for a while in water.

Sprout: To soak beans, seeds, grains or nuts in order to begin the germination process.

Stock: A flavoured liquid for soups or sauces.

Tamari: This naturally brewed sauce is made primarily from soy beans. It has a rich aroma and a smooth, balanced taste.

Tahini: A ground paste made from sesame seeds.

Wakame: A type of seaweed.

Zest: Coloured outer ring of citrus fruit.

Recommended Reading

Sprouts – the Miracle Food by Steve Meyerowitz
Enzyme Nutrition by Dr. Edward Howell
Living Food for Optimum Health by Brian Clement
You Can Heal Your Self - I Did! by Gabrielle Kirby
The Choice by Bernadette Bohan
The Choice - the Programme by Bernadette Bohan
Healthful Cuisine by Anna Maria Clement, Ph.D., N.M.D. and Chef Kelly Serbonich